INNER PEACE IN A BUSY WORLD

Dedication

To the members of the Meditation Club of the West San Gabriel Valley Boys and Girls Club, who inspired me to write this book

"How has meditation helped you?" *

Meditation has affected my life in a lot of ways. For example, my grades have dramatically improved. I meditate every two days, it helps me so much. Whenever I am stressing on a homework test, if I meditate the same day I will feel more confident, and relaxed. My test scores were normally B and C's, but now they are A's. I love to meditate, and I am [sic] probably do it for the rest of my life.

Oliver, age 13

Since I have been in meditation it is has helped me improve in many ways. One of the main things is that I am extremely more calm. Meditation helps me focus more, and with that I have better study habits. I believe that with me continuing meditation will become a habit. A habit that will help improve my life and hopefully others in a positive way.

Alex, age 14

Meditation has helped me with my school work...[It] has been a great experience for me.

Kathleen, age 12

Meditation helped me a lot with my homework. I am doing much better with my grades...
I will try to do meditation every day to improve myself.

Johnathan, age 13

What I benefit from meditation is my grades. Ever since fifth grade my grades rose to straight A's. I also benefit [from] the curiosity of my friends. They are interested in meditation and what I do in the club.

Colleen, age 12

Meditation helps me by taking things off my mind. It lets me remove stress sometimes also. Meditation gets me relaxed to a point where I don't want it to end. It takes a lot of work to meditate for twenty minutes. So I congratulate everybody who does it!

Cassandra, age 13

* *Recent question asked of members of the Meditation Club at the West San Gabriel Valley Boys and Girls Club.*

Inner Peace in a Busy World

A Young Person's Guide to Meditation

by

Cliff Johnson

*For the mind, O Krishna, is restless, turbulent, powerful and obstinate.
To control it is as hard, it seems to me, as to control the wind.*
--Bhagavad Gita

authorHOUSE®

AuthorHouse™
1663 Liberty Drive, Suite 200
Bloomington, IN 47403
www.authorhouse.com
Phone: 1-800-839-8640
This book is a work of non-fiction. Unless otherwise noted, the author and the publisher make no explicit guarantees as to the accuracy of the information contained in this book and in some cases, names of people and places have been altered to protect their privacy.

© 2007 Cliff Johnson. All rights reserved.

No part of this book may be reproduced, stored in a retrieval system, or transmitted by any means without the written permission of the author.

First published by AuthorHouse 9/6/2007

ISBN: 978-1-4343-1193-1 (sc)

To contact author:
Cliff Johnson
Quest@pacificnet.net

Printed in the United States of America
Bloomington, Indiana

This book is printed on acid-free paper.

Contents

I. Let's Get Started 1
II. What *Is* Meditation? 5
III. Types of Meditation 11
IV. Training the Body and Mind 21
V. Questions and Answers 47

All the wonders you seek are within yourself.
Sir Thomas Browne

I. Let's Get Started...

Those of you who have chosen to learn to meditate will be shortly embarking on an exciting journey. No matter what we might learn from studying the world that we see and experience every day, how many know of another world? I mean the world *inside* us. Science studies the outer world, and it is a necessary study, for it has brought us many wonderful discoveries such as electricity, the telephone, the curing of diseases, and any number of other things. These have made our lives richer and more productive. But is there any guarantee that these things will ultimately make our lives peaceful or even happy?

Yes, the world is an exciting place, but it can also be a stressful one. All of us want to succeed in one thing or another, don't we? It may be better grades, a chance to earn some extra money, the making of new friends or whatever else we discover that will enrich our lives. And what happens when you fail to reach one of these goals? Disappointment, often unhappiness, and maybe even depression.

We foolishly think that if we don't get something (and usually it is just that–a "thing") we are going to be miserable. Well, if for some reason, you don't get that thing, rest assured, you will not be miserable for long. In fact, you might find that it was not necessary after all! Instead you may just discover something of *real* value. This parable is a good example:

There was once a king long ago who had a wise advisor by the name of Nasrudin. The king had heard tales of wise men and sages who could work miracles. He sent Nasrudin out of the kingdom to report on their teachings. After sometime, Nasrudin returned and appeared before the king. "Well?" said the king. "Carrots" was the only answer of Nasrudin.

The king was furious. "Explain yourself!" he barked at Nasrudin.

"Well, your majesty, as you know the best part of the carrot is buried underground. But one must work to unearth it or it will deteriorate. Donkeys and fools are content with the green leaves above ground. They never dig out the carrot." The king laughed and told Nasrudin that he had given him the correct answer.

Meditation as a way of discovering that carrot. Only we do the digging with our minds, not a spade. In other words, for a few minutes, to start with, we leave that world outside and go *inside* to a place of peace and quiet. We look into the nature of our own minds. Let's begin the search for that carrot of wisdom now!

Is that a hand raised? "Hey, I don't know about that! I find my mind sometimes gives me all kinds of trouble. It's filled with unpleasant, sometimes painful, thoughts. When I play a video game, go shopping with my friends, or watch a movie, I can avoid those thoughts. It makes me forget things that make me sad or even angry."

You're right! These are what we call distractions, and everyone engages in them. Young people *and* adults. After all, adults are the ones who create most of them!

What we will learn to do in meditation is how to still enjoy those "things" but not be *attached* to them. Learn to take 'em or leave 'em. And, even more important, find a kind of peace and happiness in your life that you may have never known before.

This may be a good place to say a few things about *attachments*. We all have them. We are attached to our friends (and we have some special ones, don't we?), places we love to visit and spend time, even certain kinds of food and, of course, (for you girls), perhaps that latest outfit or those cute earrings you've always longed for. How about the latest boy or girl friend?

Where do we begin? You will see that this book is broken up into sections. The first section will be about some basic rules that a sincere meditator should follow if he or she is to succeed. You notice I said "should" and not "must." This is very important. Because it will be up to you to follow certain practices that will make you a successful meditator. Well, now that we have laid the groundwork of what meditation is all about, shouldn't we get started?

II. What *Is* Meditation?

Most of us are busy in the world. We have an education to pursue, we work at jobs, we also incur obligations that take a great deal of our time. We also have things we enjoy. We go to movies, watch television, use the computer, chat with our friends on the phone–and even read a good book now and then. These activities have one thing in common: they create a *very* crowded mind! And if you have ever been in a crowd, a really big, active, angry, pushing crowd, there is one thing you want to do, don't you? Get out of it!

Meditation is a way out; a way out of the crowded thoughts, activities and disturbances and trivialities that we mentioned earlier and can often make our lives discontented. When we are too busy with all those thoughts and activities that crowd in upon us, how is it possible to be happy? And we all want to be happy and at peace. Everyone does.

Inner Peace in a Busy World

Picture your mind as a huge room. Now imagine this room filled with a lot of people talking, a television on the wall noisily projecting images, a band playing in the center, and...well, you get the idea. Chaos! How can you think in such a room? How can you be at peace there? You simply can't.

Now, imagine another room that is totally empty. Its walls are painted a beautiful, restful color and there is a soft carpet on the floor. It is absolutely silent there. Not a sound. Next, see yourself sitting alone in that room with eyes closed. You are completely at peace. You have never felt such quiet, such inner silence. Then, ever so softly, you hear the sound OM. (We'll talk about that later.) It seems to come from nowhere; it fills the room with its gentle resonance. All thoughts that have disturbed and even frightened you fall away as the sound OM enters inside you and replaces all those thoughts that have caused you so much trouble.

Meditation is learning to create that quiet inner space and, through practice, control the disturbances we all face in the outside world. That is one part of meditation–*control*.

Through practice we learn to *control* what enters our mind, what we want to keep there, and what we want to release. Later we will learn how to go about this, but for now we have to recognize that the mind *under our own conscious control* is the happy mind.

A holy man once compared the uncontrolled mind to a monkey that is drunk and stung by a scorpion! Imagine how wild that monkey must have behaved. In fact, some have used the term "monkey mind" to describe the state of tumbling thoughts and countless ideas that race through our mind every day. Meditation is a means to control that "monkey mind."

Meditation involves *concentration.* Many years ago I became interested in bird watching. Of course, it involved trekking over lots of rough ground, often very early in the morning when I would have preferred to be in bed. However, it had one great joy. When my binoculars would sweep over the landscape and then... suddenly, there was that meadow lark I had been looking for all morning! My attention was focused totally on that beautiful bird. *Totally* concentrated. Nothing else existed for me at that moment in time. Every bird watcher will tell you what a joy that can be.

When your mind is able to concentrate with single-pointedness on an object, in that concentration is inner delight. Why? Because for that brief moment, distractions have literally disappeared. When that happens, the joy that is seated in your heart, just waiting to be known, pours out.

At this point, you may begin to realize there is a relationship between control of our minds and concentration. And you are right. It is impossible to truly concentrate unless we have control of our minds. Can you imagine being able to focus on a single object when you have friends talking to you all at once or the phone rings just as you are starting to prepare breakfast or open a book to read? Impossible! To meditate you need the right place *and* the right time. At least in the beginning. Later, you can learn to meditate at any time and anywhere. For now, recall that wonderful empty room with its silence except for the soft sound of OM. To meditate properly, this is the condition we must learn to create in our minds.

We should say one more thing about disturbing thoughts and how meditation helps to overcome them. In schoolrooms many years ago, desks contained small ink wells for students to dip their writing pens. No ballpoint pens in those days! Now if you were to drip water in one of those inkwells, drip by drip, what would happen to the ink? Slowly but surely water would eventually replace the ink, would it not? The inkwell would be crystal clear.

That is what meditation is really all about–replacing thoughts that are distracting, disturbing and even harmful with pure, beneficial, and happy ones. Let us see how we do this.

III. Types of Meditation

There are almost as many types of meditation as there are types of individuals. We come into the world as distinct personalities. Some of us are emotional and may weep for almost any reason. Others–they may be the so-called strong, silent type–rarely shed a tear. Most of us are somewhere in between. We may cry one minute and be tough as nails the next.

Regardless of what personality type you might be, everyone of us must deal with events that cross our path–pleasant or unpleasant. We all have them. One of the purposes of meditation is to let us look at the world in a new and better light. How? *When we control that inside world–our mind–we learn to control the world outside!* And one way of doing this is to be very, very careful what part of that outside world we let into our inner world. Remember that quiet room, painted in beautiful, restful colors? We would not want to introduce anything into that room that would disturb its peace and tranquillity, for the same reason you would not play rock music in a quiet garden. Everything has its place. It's only when things are "out of place" that we sense things to be "wrong." Following are some types of meditation to help us keep things in their right mental place.

Breath Meditation I

The one thing that all of us do every moment of our lives is breathe. Somewhere between twenty and twenty-five times a minute. One type of meditation that is practiced almost universally is breath meditation. Long ago teachers of meditation learned that breathing–other than keeping us alive by bringing oxygen to our lungs–can be a wonderful vehicle for the mind as well. In other words, they tell us, as we breathe in and out why not train the mind to concentrate on the breath as it goes through this cycle of inhalation and exhalation?

Do we just breathe and call that meditation? Not quite. We concentrate on the breath as it inhales, then concentrate again as it exhales. *We simply concentrate on the breath.* That is all. Someone once described this type of meditation as "listening to the silence between thoughts." And we all have thoughts. Lots of them. In a way, we are "thought machines." But if we can learn to find that "silence" between all those crazy, mixed-up thoughts that move through our minds, by focusing on the breath, the thoughts will grow fewer and fewer, and we will start to control and enjoy that peaceful "inside world" we talked about.

Breath Meditation II

If we choose, we can add another dimension to our breathing. We can add sound. A special kind of sound. I like to call it "silent sound." Now that is really strange, isn't it! How can sound, which by its very nature is something the ears "hear," also be silent?

Let me explain. As we breathe we can also silently chant a word or words that bring forth peace and quietness within us. One of the most powerful words or sounds is OM. We mentioned this earlier. This word, if we can call it that, has been called the source of all sounds. We find this is true when we discover this sound begins from the back of the throat and finishes with the lips together. Try it. Close your eyes, take a deep breath, open your mouth wide and then let the sound OM slowly and fully emerge with the breath, ending with your lips firmly together. Do this a few times and you will notice how your mind will begin to settle down and become peaceful.

In our meditation group we make the practice of audibly chanting OM three times before beginning our meditation. We then chant it silently as we inhale and OM as we exhale. Make sure that the beginning O-o-o-o-m is equally as long as M-m-m-m-m. Even though you cannot hear the sounds of the two words, you will find that the effect is the same as chanting them aloud. In fact, with practice you will discover that silent chanting is even more effective then chanting aloud. Your mind, in a sense, becomes your "inner ear" and as you chant silently OM seems to flow throughout your body.

Meditation on an Object

Another type of meditation found in many spiritual traditions is to concentrate on a object that you cherish or find elevating. This may be a spiritual personality, a person you revere or simply a light, usually from a candle or other source. Now we shift our focus from the breath to that of an object. Since the heart is normally considered the seat of our emotions, this is an excellent place to concentrate upon. Visualize that object in your heart. At the same time, you can chant the word or words that you use in the breath meditation. So now we not only have a word but also a form to reinforce our concentration.

What object should you meditate on? Let us touch on this briefly. Many of you have been brought up in a religious tradition. You may feel close to Christ or Buddha or some other holy personality. You may be drawn to Mother Teresa, the Dalai Lama or anyone that you revere. Or you may wish to select a beautiful flower or even a lighted candle. Mentally place that person or object into the region of your heart and concentrate there.

We can say something here about the heart region. Although we certainly know that the brain is really the main control center of our body, don't we find ourselves placing our hand over our hearts when we pledge allegiance to the flag or make any reference to ourselves? Perhaps that is the reason for the famous slogan, "Home is where the heart is." Somehow we sense that this is the center of our being. This is me! For this reason, it is a good place to position our attention in meditation.

Homing in on OM

Let us say something more about OM. We start by opening our mouth wide and let the sound start deep in our throats as we slowly close our lips for the final M-m-m-m. It is a very ancient sound that is found in many Eastern religions to begin or end a prayer. You will remember we use it in our breath meditation. Why? Because, as we said before, this is an excellent sound to calm the mind and make it peaceful.

Many years ago, I was involved in a survey of classes in comparative religion across the United States. We wanted to find out just what students in these classes considered to be really important. We offered them a list of choices such as power, money, family life, position in society, and peace and asked them to list these things in order of importance. Peace won hands down. It was number one in importance in their lives compared to all the other options.

In the tradition of the East, OM is so much a part of the culture that it begins or ends nearly every chant or prayer. It is as though an individual is called to use this soft, vibrant sound to make the shift from a turbulent mental state into a kinder, quieter one. Sometimes OM is simply chanted by worshipers for an hour or longer. In this way, the mind slowly moves into a state of peace and inner calm. When you feel restless or angry, stop and chant it either silently or aloud and let this wonderful sound help to bring your mind back into balance.

A Short Guide to Meditation

Here is a nice story from the Zen tradition:

When the mystic came down from the
mountain he was accosted by the
skeptic, who said sarcastically,
"What did you bring us from that
garden of delights you were in?"

The mystic replied, "I had every
intention of filling my hands with
flowers and giving them to my
friends on my return.
But while I was there
I became so intoxicated with the fragrance of the garden
that my hands opened and I dropped them."

This little story tells us perhaps more than any other what it is to be "carefree." Why did the mystic drop the flowers he was going to take to his friends? Because something better or higher moved his mind into a new and wonderful state. He became truly free of caring about bringing those flowers back to his friends. You could say, "Hey, that sounds pretty selfish to me! He seems to be thinking more about himself than his friends."

Well, in one sense you are right. But in another, higher sense, he did the right thing. Don't you think whatever he experienced in the garden would be communicated to his friends by his changed personality and behavior? We know that we feel happier and at ease among certain people and uncomfortable and ill at ease among others. Why? Because people that we like and feel joyful in being around often bring us something from *within themselves* that at first we may not easily recognize.

As we grow older we soon begin to learn that it is the nonmaterial things, like the hug from a close friend or the support and love from our family when we most need it, that prove to be the most important... and lasting events in our lives. These are the truly important things in life. They cost us very little– perhaps nothing at all. But throughout our life they will provide us with its greatest riches.

A Mindfulness Exercise

Here is a good exercise to remember when you feel distracted. When everything just doesn't seem to be going right, when so many things are happening around you that you don't know what to do next. You would like to pull your mind away from all those concerns, but they seem to just hang on. This is how we can learn to drop them

First, concentrate on just your hand. That's right, your hand. Next, pick up a pen. Watch your hand pick up it up with full concentration. Don't let any other thought intervene. Concentrate on your fingers grasping the pen, see how they curl around the barrel, notice where they are placed, how many fingers are holding the pen. *Be fully aware of every movement of your hand as it holds that pen.* Within a short time, your mind begins to calm down.

After you practice this exercise for some time, you can use it on other parts of your body–concentrating your full attention on your feet, legs, arms, neck and so forth.

We have used this technique at the Meditation Club either before or after our meditation session. We begin by lying lie flat on the floor. We focus our attention first at the feet, mentally instructing them to relax, next the ankles, legs and so forth until we reach the top of the head. Usually an instructor issues these "commands," but you can do it yourself. The important thing is to fully concentrate on each part of your body. And relax!

IV. Training the Body and Mind

Posture

I am certain we can all recall our parents or a teacher (if we had a particularly strict one) telling us to "Sit up straight, Johnny (or Mary)!" Let's admit it. There is something kind of pleasurable about slumping. For some reason, that nice, easy slide down the chair seems oh, so relaxing. Sitting up straight, with our back flat against the back of the chair is–well, just not very *comfortable*! Let's see if we can find a new type of comfort.

To effectively learn to meditate, it is important to acquire new habits. The rewards are well worth it. And we will find a *new* type of comfort that comes with a happy mind. Posture is important because something happens to the mind when we are sitting erect. Thousands of years ago, sages in India discovered that spiritual energy moves upward through a subtle canal in our spine. When we meditate properly, when we are concentrated, energy moves more easily up that canal. If we are bent over, it makes this energy more difficult to move through us.

Science has known for some time that we are not simply a body *and* a mind, but a body/mind. In other words, our mind is so intimately connected to our limbs, nerves, organs, circulation and other parts of our body that you could almost say they are *one*. Well, not quite. It is more like a mutual dependence. But a necessary one.

We say that someone has excellent hand/eye coordination. We can also say the same thing about mind/body coordination. I am sure you have heard of *psychosomatic* illnesses. These are illnesses or pains that directly relate to the condition of our mind. When we are upset, usually for a long period of time, the body can–and usually does–rebel. We can get sick–really sick! In other words, *what we think can directly affect our body!* Meditation is a wonderful medicine for feeling good and staying healthy.

You are probably young enough to sit cross-legged without too much discomfort. Find a pillow that is firm and use it only for meditation. The easiest posture is to simply tuck the feet under your knees. Your hands can be placed on your lap, usually with the right hand on top of the left. Or you can rest the hands on your knees with the thumb and forefinger touching. If you find this type of sitting uncomfortable for one reason or another, find a straight-back chair. Be sure and keep your feet flat on the floor. *Always* remove your shoes. Keep your eyes closed. If you are concerned about how long to meditate, have a clock or watch handy to remind you when to stop. Hey, if you forget to look at the clock–great!

Cleanliness

"Cleanliness is next to godliness." We all remember that expression. And most have just as quickly forgotten it! However, there is usually a degree of wisdom in those platitudes. That's why they have been around for ever and ever. Let's change this one to something a bit more appropriate for these pages: "Cleanliness is next to mindfulness." This is why: the mind plays all kinds of tricks on us. Let us say that you plan to meditate every evening at six–hopefully in the morning as well. Now that mind of yours could be telling you (you know, that little voice of temptation inside): "Why meditate? You can always do that later. A video game is a lot more fun. Hey, you never did return Mary's call. You need to relax, anyway." Fight these little temptations. The rewards are worth it!

A simple thing like a bath or shower before meditating not only revitalizes you but can help to silence that little voice of temptation. If you do not have time for a bath, just washing your face and hands is a help. Physical cleanliness is just another small but important device in getting your mind ready for meditation. You are about to enter the temple of your mind; step into it with a clean and refreshed body.

Promptness

Whenever possible start your meditation at the time you have agreed to start. In our own meditation group, we begin precisely because the group comes to expect their meditation to begin at that *precise* time. And the *mind* of the meditator comes to expect it as well. A friend of mine told me a story that illustrates this. He made an appointment with a well-known spiritual teacher. "I am able to give you exactly one hour of my time. Please tell me how I can help you."

The teacher brought with him an alarm clock which he set at one hour. When one hour had elapsed, the teacher rose, politely said that he hoped he had been of help and left the room. My friend said that the promptness of the teacher's arrival and departure made a deep impression on him. It permitted him to focus his attention on what was bothering him, since he knew he had only a limited amount of time, and this greatly aided in solving his mental problem.

Procrastination. We all put things off from one time to another. Why do we put things off for a later time (and that "later time" may never come!)? It may be something we just don't want to face. The classic "putting off" thing you probably do is homework. Why? Because in most cases, unless you really "love" that subject, it's *hard* work. In other words, we procrastinate doing things that are unpleasant. Or things that we feel might cause us embarrassment or failure. One famous psychiatrist said that a turning point came in his life when he decided to do the things he hated to do first. Then he could relax and enjoy doing the more pleasant ones. In other words, don't put off until tomorrow what you know you should do today!

Also, when we do things promptly, we won't have to worry about being embarrassed or failing. We spend our mental energy in making sure we get to that place on time or do what is required of us at the time we agree to. Ask employers what they most value in an employee and most will tell you *dependability*. In other words: being at the right place at the right time. What is the real reward for this promptness? Success in your school work, your job, your relationship with others. *Do what you say you will do.*

Remember that term, "Johnny on the spot"? I always like it because to me it means a guy or a gal who has a lot of energy and who is right there–on the spot–the place where you expect them to be at the time they say they will be there. You may just find it's not all that bad to be the early bird. Remember. It gets the worm!

What I have just written reminds me of a story I think worth telling. It's a true story about a now-famous man who could be described as a "Johnny on the spot" type. During one summer during his college career, he took a job as a bellhop (as they are known) in a large, fancy hotel in upper state New York, handling the bags of incoming and outgoing guests. It is, of course, traditional to tip the bell hop for this service. What impressed the guests was that this young man refused any sort of tip for his services. He told them he did not feel his job required extra compensation.

He said he was pleased to do it without additional reward. Needless to say, this so impressed many of those he served that when the summer was over, he had numerous job offers. His career was off to a running start!

Regularity of Practice

There is nothing more creative than meditation. Why? Because you are forming inside you a new and fresh YOU! A better, happier, and more fulfilled you. The best way to do this is to form good meditation habits. We do this by establishing a specific time, whenever possible, for our meditation and sticking to it.

What are these times? Morning is best. This doesn't mean you have to get up at 4 a.m. But most of us are fresher in the morning (if you didn't watch the late, late show). Whatever time you choose, try to be consistent in following that schedule. Most of you know how easy it is to grab the TV remote (and we've all done this) instead of a textbook to prepare for tomorrow's test.

Sticking to a meditation schedule is much the same thing as preparing for that test. Once the mind knows that you are serious it has a way of slowly (ever so slowly) obeying you and saying, "Okay, it's time to meditate. I'll give you your twenty minutes." We'll get into the other times of meditation later. For now, try to keep to a regular schedule. It's worth it.

Neatness

How many times have you heard your mother tell you: "Clean up that room of yours. It's a mess!" It's happened to all of us. Neatness or caring for one's personal appearance and the environment in which we live, study, eat, work–and especially meditate–is important if we are to enjoy a happy, peaceful mind.

When we organized our Meditation Club, the first rule we agreed upon was that the shoes of the meditation students be lined up parallel to one another, toes touching the wall outside the room. We *never* wear shoes inside the meditation room. It is quite a sight to see shoes of all different descriptions lined up like little soldiers!

Why do we do this? On the surface it might seem kind of silly. I mean, we put on and take off our shoes several times a day. Isn't the most important thing we should be concerned with is what happens *inside* the meditation room, when we really sit down to meditate? Not really. When runners get ready for the big race, what is the first thing they do? They stretch, they run up and down in place, and may even find a quiet place to go to settle their mind and think hard about winning. This is called *preparation*. The same goes for preparing for a final exam or any examination for that matter–reviewing notes, cracking that textbook for a final look or asking friends for some help. Our simple act of lining up our shoes before we meditate is also a kind of preparation. We organize our shoes. With that simple ritual, we are getting ready to organize our mind through concentration. We are getting ready to meditate.

Now, we have to accept the simple fact that some people are just plain neater and better organized than others. They are the "neatos." They are in every class, in every party, well...just about everywhere there are people! We've all known them. They *always* have their pencils sharpened (usually two or three), they are *always* smartly dressed, *always* organized...and so on. If you are one, well, you may not feel it necessary to read any further.

However, when we talk about the discipline of neatness, we do not mean *obsessive* neatness. That is a kind of illness. In fact, an obsession of any kind is never healthy. If you are obsessive about anything, you will most likely never develop a meditative mind. You will be too concerned about your obsession! The neatness we are talking about is being *aware* of the care of your body and mind. Making sure that the space you live and meditate in reflects the mind that you meditate with. It's a simple formula. And it works.

One of the fundamental beliefs in Eastern thought is that *the mind takes on the form of that which it concentrates upon.* In simple language, this means that we basically are what we think. Someone once said to his teacher, "You know, when I have taken my shower, my room is well-ordered, and everything is in its place–well, I think better! I concentrate better!" The teacher told him that this was a perfect example of that earlier idea: his mind was taking on the "form" of his environment. It was getting organized, getting concentrated *and* getting ready to meditate!

You can try almost anything that helps you meditate better. I like to use what in India is known as a *chaddar*–just another name for a shawl. If you are a girl, you might want a pretty one with attractive colors and patterns. You fellows are not going to be concerned with that. The *chaddar* serves a couple of important services. The most important one is that it reminds you every time you use it that you are going to sit down, concentrate and begin your meditation. For this reason, you should not use it for any other purpose.

I have had my own *chaddar* for more than thirty years and have gotten so accustomed to it that I always feel a bit at a loss if I mediate without it. In our Meditation Club we do not use *chaddars*, but another reminder. We wear bright orange t-shirts with a symbol of the sun imprinted on the back. It is just one more help in keeping the mind focused.

Curb That Tongue!

We love to talk! Do we ever! There is a famous Zen saying that goes like this: "He who speaks does not know; he who knows does not speak." Now, how do you ask a teenager to get off the phone when he or she is about to take in a juicy bit of gossip? Well, you know–who has just broken up with whom. Then there is the classmate who asks you, "What was your grade on the final?" And have you noticed how the person that *always* asks that question is generally the one who got the "A"?

There is nothing wrong with a healthy exchange of talk between people. As humans we are the only species with the wonderful capacity to express ourselves through speech. However, sometimes we take it a bit too far. We overstretch it.

Someone I know told me that he really found it hard to like a particular person I know because "he always speaks without paragraphs!" What did he mean by that? Well, if you paid attention to your English teacher, you know that a paragraph has a topic sentence that expresses its main idea or theme. Then follow other sentences, long or short, that develop that idea. One paragraph is tied to another until you finish the essay or whatever else you were writing or reading.

However, there is always a break between paragraphs. You can see I am doing this now in this section. What if I ran all my paragraphs and sentences together? It would be one big, unintelligible mess, wouldn't it? You know the expression, "I couldn't get a word in edgewise?" That's the way our friend talked. And the result? You were so concentrated on wishing him to slow down and pause for a bit that you never listened to or absorbed a word he said!

Learning to remain silent is not easy. Nearly everyone has an opinion about something or other, and we are usually eager to express those opinions. Here are a few rules to remember when it comes to speaking:

1. If you think what you are about to say will injure someone, don't say it.
2. Tell the truth–but never a harsh truth.

3. Try to listen first and speak later.
4. If you are angry, count to ten before you react.
5. People who speak the fewest words are often those whom others listen to the most.

There is something else we should mention. It's what nearly everyone does and most do without thinking of the possible damage it can cause. I am talking about–you guessed it–gossip! Haven't we all listened to it (and engaged in it)? "You'll never guess what Cynthia said about John? Okay, I'll tell you, but promise you won't breathe a word to anyone else!" You can be sure she (or he) will! On the surface, gossip seems innocent enough. After all, in most cases it is not vicious or hateful information you are sharing with your friends. Just some little juicy bit of information. What *real* harm can that do? Now I want you to imagine that *you* are the subject of that gossip. That it is *you* they are talking about with such apparent enjoyment. It wouldn't be very pleasant would it?

Someone very wise once wrote that before we speak our words should leave through three gates. At the first gate we ask ourselves, "Are these words true?" If so, let me pass on; if not, then go back.

At the second gate, we ask, "Are they necessary?" In other words, do they help someone? Or only cause injury?

At the last gate we ask, "Are they kind." If we still feel we must speak out, we need to choose words that are supporting and loving, not words that wound or embarrass someone.

There was a famous French movie produced many years ago. It started out with two people who knew each other. After a while, they parted. One of them met someone else and started a bit of gossip about the person whom he had just left. That person next met someone and reported what she *thought* she had heard to her friend. Since she didn't much care for that person, she added a few of her own "facts." In time, the same information went through eight different groups. Eventually, it got back to the subject of the rumor–completely changed! Imagine how she felt! There is an old expression, "Keep it under your hat!" Well, not too many of us wear hats anymore, but the meaning is the same. I guess I have to again bring up one of the favorite sayings of a friend of mine, "If it's not worth saying, don't say it at all."

Mental Cleanliness

"The mind is everything," said a sage many years ago. It is a precious instrument and one that deserves our greatest care and attention. Can you imagine functioning without a mind? Impossible. Another Chinese sage, Lao Tse, once wrote: "The world surrenders to a mind that is still." In other words, a meditative mind.

Let us take a brief look at our mind. What is it? Well, it is certainly the main engine of our being, isn't it? This book could well have been titled *A Guide to Controlling the Mind*, because meditation *is* just that–controlling and using our mind to find levels of inner peace and happiness not available to us if we are constantly drawn outside of ourselves and concerned only with things of passing interest.

When we talk about "mental cleanliness," we are talking about mental housekeeping. What does a good housekeeper do? Well, if you were raised in my mother's house, you would know what that means! Her house was a thing to behold. Carpet vacuumed like clockwork, dishes *always* dried and put neatly away, beds made without a crease–well, that was my second-generation Dutch mother. Why can't we treat our minds the same way? Of course, the purpose of this book is not to make us into expert housekeepers.

At the same time, we may just find that we *will* keep a better house or cleaner room if we do a little mental housekeeping.

It has been said that the world is simply a reflection of our mind. What does this mean? We all know people who, no matter what you say to them, take everything "the wrong way." You express to them something you believe to be a compliment. They view it as just the opposite. "You know, Mary, I really like what Susie has done with her hair."

Instead of agreement we get something like: "Sure you do! Don't kid me! You really think it came out of a bottle, don't you?" This is just one example of how *your* mind reacts much differently from *Mary's* mind. Both of you saw Susie's hair but made different decisions about it. Why? Most likely because of what each of you brought into the decision-making process. In other words, why one of you liked the hair and the other didn't. And what it really boils down to (and we know this, don't we) is whether or not we like Susie!

What we are leading up to here, in sort of a roundabout way, is that everything that enters the mind through our eyes, ears and other senses creates an *impression*. If enough of these impressions of the same kind enter the mind over a period of time, we

A Short Guide to Meditation

have what we call a *tendency* or disposition to act or think in a certain way.

Let's look at the above example of your and Mary's attitude toward Susie and her hair. It would appear obvious that you and Mary have experienced different reactions to Susie because of the different impressions influencing your reaction to her. Perhaps Mary and Susie got into an argument months back. Each angry word spoken and perhaps a shove or two– all have gone to create impressions and eventually a tendency or inclination to create dislike, perhaps even hatred, between the two of them. Do we want this? Of course not.

As meditators we must be particularly careful *to keep our minds as free as possible from these negative impressions.* We now live in a world surrounded by all kinds of influences that constantly invade our senses- television, cell phones, ipods, movies, advertising, and a whole host of other sights, sounds and smells.

Since it is growing in prevalence, and without many legal restrictions, a word or two must be said about pornography. This is a particularly dangerous phenomenon (for lack of a better word) to anyone who cherishes an uncluttered, peaceful mind. Expressed simply, *the exposure to pornography drags the mind down.* I can't think of any other way to say it. As meditators, we want to pull the mind up! And keep it up! People who watch pornography or waste their valuable hours in reading books of similar content can never be happy or peaceful.

And that's why we meditate, isn't it?

Worry

"Worry, worry go away and come back some other day." We all remember that rhyme. Unfortunately, worry will be sure to come back to us–if we don't know how to handle it.

We all have an idea what worry is. More specifically, the dictionary defines it as a "troubled mind arising from the frets and cares of life." Well, that tells us *what* worry is, but does it tell us what causes it?

The primary cause of worry is *fear*. This could be a fear of criticism by your friends, fear that you may not pass that class or classes, fear of not being liked, fear of the future or any number of anxieties that can make your life really miserable! Worry makes meditation difficult. For as soon as you try to concentrate--*wham*! Here comes that fear, that anxiety. You simply can't concentrate. You're concentrating on the *what* that is worrying you! So, *what* do you do about it?

The first thing to remember is that what you are fearing (which is creating all that worry) is in the vast majority of cases, simply *without any foundation.* In most cases, it is the result of your own imagination. I'll tell you my own experience with worry.

I am a contractor, and some months back I sent an estimate for a large work order to one of my clients. Assuming it was approved (since he was an established client), I thought no more about it and actually started to do the work. A week or so passed and I contacted him. He was furious that I had started work without his approval, and said he was thinking about finding someone else. I suddenly discovered I had sent the estimate to the wrong fax number! Although I explained my error and offered to meet with him, he refused. Several more weeks passed, and I confess I was worried! This was a main source of my income. I grew increasingly concerned, certain I would lose the job. As it turned out, he was simply busy and had earlier accepted my explanation. He just hadn't notified me. My worry was for nothing.

Situations that might seem hopeless at first will usually find a reasonable and happy solution. Did she (or he) not return your smile or turn away when you approached? More than likely you're not the cause. There's a good chance an earlier argument with mom over breakfast might be the real culprit. Smile first the next time. You can bet it will be returned.

Years ago, there was a famous essay called "You are not the target." It asked us to remember that quite often when people direct their anger at us it is often intended for someone else–someone that person, for one reason or another, cannot contend with. It may be a boss, a parent, an older brother or sister. And if you are not the real cause, should you worry about it?

The following advice of the Dalai Lama seems to say it all: "Never worry about things you can't change. Nor should you worry about things you can change. Just do what you have to do to make the changes. Don't worry about the results."

Str-e-e-e-tching the Truth

"I swear to tell the truth, the whole truth and nothing but the truth." Even if you have never been in a courtroom, you have certainly heard these words in many TV dramas or movies with courtroom scenes. Not only does the law value the importance of truth telling, but almost anyone that *you* value does as well. You can be sure you'll not have many friends if you get an unpleasant reputation of one who cannot be depended upon to tell the truth.

In our earlier section on gossip, we talked about a *type* of lying, for lack of a better way to express it, that is forgivable. This sort of lying was expressed by a wise man many years ago: "One should always tell the truth, *but never a harsh truth.*" Here is an example. Many years ago, my spiritual teacher was giving a lecture. At the close of the talk, as was his habit, he always greeted members of the audience at the door. One woman approached him wearing a particularly large, ugly hat. A bright red feather protruded from it.

"What do you think of my new hat, Swami?" she asked. He knew he could not lie and tell the woman his true feelings about the hat. That would be a hurtful truth. However, he did find one part of the hat that was not all that unattractive. He answered with a smile, "Madam, that is a beautiful feather!"

Giving evidence in court is one kind of truth, in which we are expected to tell the truth no matter how painful it might be. Another is speaking our minds truthfully to others, but not hurting or injuring them. There are always ways to speak honestly without being dishonest or offensive. As you continue in your meditation, you will discover that things you formerly could keep buried in that very, very deep "well of forgetfulness" will slowly start to come out. In some ways, this is a good thing. You are beginning to rid yourself of a lot of negative "stuff" that does not contribute to a healthy mind.

Remember that example of the inkwell? How the ink is slowly replaced by water, drip by drip, until it is completely gone? That is how meditation operates in our mind. If we have the habit of lying, we slowly, but ever so slowly, keep adding more ink in the form of deceit or untruth to that inkwell. Our mind becomes so filled with lies and negative influences that those clear drops of water from our meditation will have a tough job indeed to replace the ink! So, the next time you think about spreading that unfounded rumor or telling that "little white lie" (which is *never* really white!), think about that inkwell. Let those drops of concentrated, kind and honest thoughts do their job of clarifying and purifying your mind!

Aids to Meditation

1. A place to meditate

This may not always be so easy to find. If you live in a big house, you might be able to locate some corner to call your own (a large closet would be great!) to be used only for meditation. If you are adventurous, there are many quiet, peaceful places to meditate–a park, a church, a walk in the woods. You can walk *and* meditate! If you are so inclined, keep with you spiritual or other books that you find helpful in concentration. When your parents learn that you are serious about being a meditator, you'll probably find them willing to help you. In fact, when the parents of one member of our group noticed her meditating every day, they decided to join her! It's catching.

2. Some helpful articles

The use of *incense*, which has been used throughout the world for many centuries—perhaps thousands of years—mostly in religious ceremonies, is a wonderful aid to meditation. One of its more common uses is simply as an air purifier. Of course, you can buy purifiers in the market in a spray can. But incense produces a fragrance that you can never find in a supermarket. Its best use, however, is to create an atmosphere of peace and sweetness and, through that kind of association, to help bring your mind into a meditative state. Incense produces a subtle influence that you can't easily define. But once you start to use it, you will never be without it. Its slender sticks come in many varied fragrances and are widely available. (My personal favorite is saffron.) You should place the stick in a simple incense holder.

If we haven't mentioned a *meditation pillow*, we should have. Be sure and get one that is *firm.* This cannot be emphasized enough. Good meditation pillows are not cheap, but if you are serious about your practice, they are well worth the price. The "Samadhi" brand is excellent and can be ordered over the internet.

Now a word or two about a shrine or altar. These words normally have a religious meaning. However, what we are referring to here is a small table of good quality, usually available for a reasonable price (Chinese merchants are noted for selling ones of all sizes). Keep your meditation table clean and polished. Here you can place your incense holder. If there is some personality you revere, place that person's photo in front of you. In some odd way, your place of meditation becomes–and I know this sounds strange–your own "little home within your home." You will grow to love it and treasure the time you sit before it.

One thing more should be mentioned. I refer to what might be called "reminders." Although members of our Meditation Club are far too young to drive, we decided to issue a different kind of license. We call it a "License to Meditate." It looks awfully much like a real license, with a photo and signature at the bottom. On the reverse side is listed "Ten Things to Remember." These are:

1. Meditate every day
2. Tell the truth, but never a harsh one
3. Always speak kindly
4. Give to those in need
5. Be friendly to all
6. Never hate anyone or anything
7. Be ready to forgive
8. If you promise–obey it
9. See the good in everyone
10. Be the first to love

In Conclusion...

Many years ago, I was warned by a professional speaker that I should never end a talk with two fatal words: "In conclusion..." He said your audience will immediately start to get ready to leave–and very quickly forget nearly all of your concluding remarks. So here I am doing just that in this book. But, please, stay with me for only a few more sentences. I promise not to keep you long. The bell is almost ready to ring...

This is not a long book. And for a reason. Meditation is, above all, "doing." You can read literally hundreds of books or scriptures on techniques and methods of meditation–with all the various ways to sit and concentrate and their accompanying disciplines. They will, after all, only point the way. It is *you* who must tread it.

With all my heart, I wish you well on your journey. It is worth it!

V. Questions and Answers

Q: Will meditation help me to make better grades?

A: Definitely! In our meditation class, we frequently ask our meditators how they are doing in school. The inevitable response is: "Great!" Our meditators report that many of their grades are improving in classes in which they were having trouble. One member told the group that in a class she was failing, she climbed to a "C." *All because she spent a few minutes in meditation each day.* The reason is that once the mind is helped to concentrate in meditation, it can be helped to concentrate in other areas as well.

Q: How do I explain to my friends or parents what I am doing? Many might believe it is strange—even weird.

A: We often think things to be strange when we don't understand them. The best way to describe meditation is that you are spending some time every day in practicing "quiet time."

Everyone understands that! This is a busy world, and if they discover you have been smart enough to find a way out of it for a few minutes a day, they will think you are smart to do so. And they may want to try meditation also!

Q: My family believes in prayer but they are not really sure what meditation is. What do I tell them?

A: You can tell them that the object of meditation is to concentrate the mind only and through that concentration to rid it of a lot of its restlessness and disturbances. Prayer is a form of concentration, but a type of expression guided by one's particular religion. Meditation is found in religion, but you are not required to be religious to practice it.

Q: I get sleepy when I try to meditate. What do I do?

A: This is a kind of an escape trick of the mind. The mind is a rebellious fellow and does not always like to be told what to do! Writers often experience this when they find themselves undergoing "writer's block." The best thing to do is get up, drink a glass of cold water or juice and sit down again to meditate. Then tell your mind: "Now I am going to meditate!" It will listen.

Q: What is the best time for meditation?

A: According to most traditions, the three best times are early morning, sunset and midnight. Most meditators settle for morning and sunset. Morning is perhaps best of all since this is when the mind is freshest. (I am sure we can say midnight is probably when our minds are sleepiest!) Sunset is the next best time because your school or work day is over. This is a good time to bring the mind within and try to remove it from the events of the day. I think most of us can depart from tradition and remain asleep at midnight!

Q: How long should one meditate?

A: When we organized our first meditation class, we started at ten minutes. Over a period of the next few weeks the periods increased to twenty minutes. Perhaps even more important in the early stages is frequency. The mind must get established in recognizing that "This is the time for my meditation." Unfortunately, our meditation club meets only once a week. But its members are encouraged to practice regularly at home or, for that matter, in any quiet place.

Q: Speaking of that, I can't seem to find a *quiet* place to meditate at home. There's just too much going on there! What do I do?

A: If you really want to meditate, almost any place can be suitable for meditation. Let's use the example of a bus ride. You can use that time of only fifteen minutes or half an hour to meditate instead of looking out the window, daydreaming or talking with a friend. In other words, there is really no time or place in which you cannot meditate. The conditions may not be perfect, but they do exist. And imperfect or not, each time we meditate we advance just a few steps more in mental clarity and peace. (Let's not forget the example of the ink well.) We soon begin to wonder how we were able to begin our day without meditating!

Okay, Let's Recap

1. Make a firm commitment to meditate regularly.
2. Find a quiet place.
3. Sit either cross-legged or in a chair. Keep the back straight.
4. Breathe in and out slowly. As you do, silently chant OM on the in breath and OM on the out breath.
5. Concentrate on a symbol you find meaningful–Christ, Buddha or a beautiful object such as a flower–and visualize that in the heart region.
6. During meditation consider the outside world as apart from you. Let it float away like a cloud.
7. When you have finished your meditation, bow and offer thanks.

**What you acquire in meditation
Spend in Love**

The Author

Cliff Johnson has been practicing meditation for more than forty years. Although raised in a Western religious tradition, an early meeting with his teacher, an Indian guru, started him on the path of meditation. A number of years later, he became strongly drawn to the spiritual life and joined the Ramakrishna Order of India as a novice monk. During this period, he served as executive editor of *Vedanta and the West* magazine, for which he wrote numerous essays. He is editor of *Vedanta: an Anthology of Hindu Scripture, Commentary, and Poetry* (Harper & Row, 1971). Though no longer a monk, Cliff continues to meditate and maintain his spiritual practices. Two years ago, he organized a nonsectarian meditation club for youngsters at a nearby Boys and Girls Club, which largely inspired this book. He is also a play writer, book editor and runs a contracting business. He lives in Studio City, California.